BiG Thoughts for Little Thinkers

The Church
By Joey Allen

New Leaf Press

First printing: June 2025

Copyright © 2025 by Joey Allen. All rights reserved. No part of this book may be reproduced, copied, broadcast, stored, or shared in any form whatsoever without written permission from the publisher, except in the case of brief quotations in articles and reviews. For information write:

New Leaf Press, P.O. Box 726, Green Forest, AR 72638

New Leaf Press is a division of the New Leaf Publishing Group, LLC.

ISBN: 978-0-89221-774-8

ISBN: 978-1-61458-932-7(digital)

Library of Congress Control Number: 2025933428

Please consider requesting that a copy of this volume be purchased by your local library system.

Printed in China

Please visit our website for other great titles: www.newleafpress.com

For information regarding promotional opportunities, please contact the publicity department at pr@nlpg.com.

Illustrations and text by Joey Allen

For my daughter Claire

FOREWORD

Amidst the demands of ministry and over the complaints of His disciples, Jesus famously declared "Let the children alone, and do not hinder them from coming to Me; for the Kingdom of Heaven belongs to such as these" (Matthew 19:14).

Jesus' heart for children must be our heart as well. Like our Lord, Christian parents and ministers should call children to Christ, introducing them to the way of the Master from early childhood. And that's important because Christ didn't say children have to become like adults to enter the Kingdom. He said adults must become like children. Characteristics like humility and dependence are essential to following Christ and are inherent in children.

Yet, our responsibility doesn't end when our children give their lives to Christ—that's where it begins. As parents and ministers, our goal must be to see our children wholistically formed in Christ, supplied with a doctrinal foundation from which their faith can mature.

In 25 years of pastoral ministry, I've become convinced that one of the church's most common and pernicious errors is underestimating how much biblical truth children can comprehend. Indeed, children can receive, believe, understand, and apply God's Word—and that should be our aim.

This conviction is why I'm thankful for Joey Allen and this collection of *Big Thoughts for Little Thinkers* books. Over the past two decades God has used these books to influence countless children for Christ. I heartily recommend this resource, believing God will use it for many decades.

Jason K. Allen, Ph.D.
President — Midwestern Baptist Theological Seminary & Spurgeon College

A WORD TO PARENTS AND TEACHERS

The Church stands in contrast to our increasingly individualistic, digital, and depersonalized world. The Church celebrates the communal, physical, and relational nature of our common faith. As Christians, we believe the same gospel message passed down from the Apostles. The same Lord Jesus Christ cleanses us, the same heavenly Father adopts us as His children, and the same Holy Spirit indwells us and unites us as brothers and sisters in the family of God. It has always been the plan of God for the people of God to gather in the presence of God and scatter the glory of God among the nations.

At church, we participate in various embodied, communal experiences: we feel the wetness of the water in baptism, and we taste, chew, and swallow the Lord's Supper. As we fellowship, we hug, shake hands, or kiss, as appropriate in different cultures. As we sing, we employ our lungs and vocal cords to join our voices with one another. As we pray, we kneel, stand with raised hands, bow our heads, or assume a number of other postures to align our bodies and hearts.

Those who say, "I can connect with God without going to church," sabotage their spiritual health, undermine their fruitfulness, and inhibit their intimacy with the Lord. They leave themselves vulnerable to doctrinal deviation, moral collapse, and relational desolation. Yes, living in community is fraught with challenges, but God designed the Church as the context where we grow into Christ likeness. Jesus Himself commanded us to love one another (John 13:34). This kind of love, according to Jesus, serves as a validation and a testimony of our identity as His disciples (John 13:35). We bless our children by implanting in their hearts a love for and commitment to God's Church.

Joey Allen
Chair of Missions and Evangalism, Midwestern Theological Seminary

Hi! My name is Josh. Everyone needs a family. God made the Church to be our spiritual family.

1 Corinthians 12:12-18; Ephesians 2:19; 1 Timothy 3:15

If you have trusted in Jesus, you are a part of the family of God, which is the worldwide Church. You share a spiritual bond with every Christian in the world.

1 Corinthians 1:2; 12:12-14; 1 Peter 2:9

A local church is a group of Christians who join together to worship God, love one another, study the Bible, grow as God's children, and make Jesus known to the world.

Acts 2:37-47; Romans 10:14-15, 2 Corinthians 5:18-21; Hebrews 10:24-25

Every Christian should be a faithful member of a church in their area, because God did not create us to be alone.

Genesis 2:18; Romans 12:4-5; 1 Corinthians 12:27

After you trust in Jesus, you should be baptized in your church. Baptism is how you show other people that you believe Jesus died on the Cross, was buried, and came back to life.

Matthew 28:19; Romans 6:4-11

At Church, Christians regularly eat the Lord's Supper together. We eat bread and drink grape juice to help us think about what Jesus did for us on the Cross and what we will celebrate in Heaven. The Lord's Supper is a special time to help us stay connected with other church members.

Matthew 26:26–29; Luke 22:14–20; 1 Corinthians 11:23–26

Church is where you learn to follow Jesus and help others follow Jesus.

Mark 1:17; John 13:34–35; Galatians 6:2

A big part of following Jesus is loving other people, and you can't do that by yourself. Christians spend time together and become close friends. They encourage one another to walk with God.

Acts 2:42-47; 1 Thessalonians 5:11; Hebrews 10:24-25

Church members take care of each other. How wonderful it is to be surrounded by people who want to provide what you need, comfort you when you're sad, and help you when you fail. The Church should be a place of love and truth.

Romans 12:15; 1 Corinthians 12:25-26; 2 Corinthians 1:3-4; Galatians 5:13; 6:2; Ephesians 4:15

When Christians gather at church, they love to sing! Singing songs that are full of truth is a great way to worship God.

Psalm 149:1-3; Ephesians 5:19; Colossians 3:16

Christians read the Bible together. The Bible tells the story of God sending Jesus and the Holy Spirit to save people from sin, defeat Satan, and make the world new and beautiful again.

John 17:17; Acts 2:1-4; 2 Timothy 2:15; 3:16-17

Studying the Bible with other Christians helps us understand it better. We learn who God is, what He has done, who we are, and how we should relate to one another. The more we know God, the more we will love Him and each other!

Romans 15:14;
Colossians 3:16;
1 Timothy 4:13;
2 Timothy 3:14-17

Church members love to pray together. Prayer is talking to God. When we pray, we tell God that we love and trust Him, tell Him we are sorry for our sins, share our troubles, ask Him to give us what we need, and thank Him for His gifts.

Psalm 62:8; Matthew 6:9-13; Luke 18:1; Acts 2:42; 1 Thessalonians 5:16-18; 1 John 1:9

Christians give their money, time, and abilities to support the church's mission, love other church members, and help the poor and hurting.

Acts 2:44-45;
1 Corinthians 16:1-2;
2 Corinthians 9:7-8

God gives every Christian—even young Christians—spiritual gifts to bless the Church. The Holy Spirit makes some members gifted at speaking and others gifted at serving. How can you use your spiritual gifts to build the Church?

Romans 12:1-8; 1 Corinthians 12; Ephesians 4:7-13; 1 Peter 4:10-11

Leaders of the church should help every member use their gifts for one another. Some leaders are called "pastors." Pastor means shepherd. Godly pastors serve the church, teach the Bible, and protect members from false teachings.

Acts 20:28; Ephesians 4:11-13; 1 Timothy 3:1-7; Titus 1:5-9; 1 Peter 5:1-5

Teachers in the church help others understand, love, and obey the Bible.

Matthew 28:19-20; Romans 12:6-7, 15:4; Ephesians 4:11-12; 1 Timothy 1:5, 5:17; 2 Timothy 2:15; Titus 2:1-8; 1 Peter 2:5

People who serve the church are sometimes called "deacons." Those who help the church tell outsiders about Jesus are called "evangelists."

Romans 16:1;
Ephesians 4:11-12;
1 Timothy 3:8-12; 1 Peter 4:10-11

Every Christian should tell others the message of Jesus. The Church's mission is to spread the message of Jesus around the world. That's why the Church sends and supports missionaries who bring the Good News to people who have never heard it.

Matthew 28:19-20; Acts 13:2-3; Romans 10:14-15; 15:20-21; 2 Timothy 4:1-5

The church works to spread Jesus' message so that more people will trust and love Him. Healthy churches should start other healthy churches and help them grow.

Acts 6:7; 8:4; 14:21-23;
1 Corinthians 3:6-7;
2 Timothy 2:2

The Bible describes the Church as a family, a flock of sheep, a bride, a building, and a body.

John 10:14-16; 1 Corinthians 12:12-14; Ephesians 2:19; 5:25-27; 1 Peter 2:5

The Church is like a family because God is our Father, and other Christians are our spiritual brothers and sisters. Church is where we learn how to get along with one another.

Psalm 133:1; Matthew 18:15–20; John 20:17; Romans 8:14–17; 12:10; 14:19; Ephesians 2:19; 1 Timothy 3:15; 1 John 4:21

The Church is like a flock of sheep, with Jesus as our shepherd. He leads, feeds, and protects us.

Psalm 23; John 10:11-18; 21:15; Hebrews 13:20; 1 Peter 5:2-4

The Church is like a bride because Jesus loves the Church and gave His life for her. He makes the Church holy and clean. Because Jesus cares for the Church, we should, too.

2 Corinthians 11:2;
Ephesians 5:22-33; Revelation 19:7-9; 21:2

The Church is like a building, with Jesus as the cornerstone and Church members as stones of the building.

1 Corinthians 3:9-17; 6:19-20; Ephesians 2:19-22; 1 Peter 2:4-7

The Church is also like a body. Each member is a part of the body, and Jesus is the head. Every member of the body must work together. When any part hurts, the whole body should try to help.

*1 Corinthians 12:12-27;
Ephesians 1:22-23, 4:15-16;
Colossians 1:18*

All of God's people will be joined together in perfect love in Heaven. In church, we practice the kind of love we will enjoy for all eternity.

John 17:20-23;
1 Peter 3:8;
1 John 4:7-12;
Revelation 21:1-6

One day, all believers from all over the world will be in Heaven for a huge party. We will worship Jesus in the Spirit to the glory of God the Father.

Philippians 2:9-11;
Revelation 5:11-14; 7:9; 19:6-9